The young HANS CHRISTIAN ANDERSEN

The young HANS CHRISTIAN ANDERSEN

By KAREN HESSE

Illustrated by

ERIK BLEGVAD

SCHOLASTIC PRESS ◆ NEW YORK

With enormous gratitude for the invisible guidance of my mother's hand,

and the gentle wisdom of Simi Berman, Erik Blegvad,

Lenore Blegvad, Eileen Christelow, Sharon Creech,

Kate and Rachel Hesse, Randy Hesse, Liza Ketchum, Elizabeth Parisi,

Leda Schubert, Laura Stevenson, Elizabeth Szabla, Wendy Watson

and, most particularly, Jean Feiwel.

Text copyright © 2005 by Karen Hesse / Illustrations copyright © 2005 by Erik Blegvad

Library of Congress Cataloging-in-Publication Data
Hesse, Karen.
The young Hans Christian Andersen / by Karen Hesse ; [illustrations by Erik Blegvad]. — 1st ed.
p. cm.   ISBN 0-439-67990-7 (hardcover : alk. paper)

1. Andersen, H. C. (Hans Christian), 1805-1875—Juvenile literature.
2. Authors, Danish—19th century—Biography—Juvenile literature. I. Blegvad, Erik. II. Title.
PT8119.H46 2005   839.8'136—dc22   [B]   2004029100

10 9 8 7 6 5 4 3 2 1   05 06 07 08 09

The text type was set in Bodoni Old Style. The display type was set in P22 Arts & Crafts Hunter.
The illustrations were done in pen and ink, and watercolors.
Book design by Elizabeth B. Parisi
Printed in Singapore 46 · First edition, October 2005

To Erik and Lenore

with love

— K.H.

"The story of the thorny path does not end as a fairy tale in bliss and happiness here on earth, it reaches out into space and into eternity."

— From "THE THORNY PATH"
by Hans Christian Andersen

The Most Incredible

◇ ·· ◇

In the town of Odense, under a velvet sky, the wind
invited the church bells to dance, it nuzzled cuckoos
dozing in their beech-trees and sleepy ducks tucked
up in their riverbeds.

Threading through Funen, past the Danish people
cozy in their quilts, the Odense River sang of a half-
timbered cottage where in one small room squeezed a
shoemaker and his wife and their brand-new son, who
was no more than a squalling stick of a thing, with toes
and fingers like little worms wriggling and a mouth
wide open like a baby stork.

THE NIGHTINGALE

Hans Christian squirmed in his swaddling clothes, his little fists locked tight, his rumpled face red as a catch of wild roses.

The vicar, pacing in his robes, shot a longing glance toward the church door, wishing to escape the sound of that howling infant. In all his years the vicar had never heard such piercing lament.

Flustered, Ane-Marie patted her baby's chest, rocking him back and forth in her arms, trying to calm him. But old Nicolas Gomar – Hans Christian's godfather – chuckled, stroking the wee boy's head with his wrinkled hand. He knew a nightingale when he heard one.

GRANDMOTHER

◇—••—◇

His grandmother tended the garden at Greyfriars Hospital where the sick, the old, and the mad nibbled away at their days. Often, while his grandmother worked, Hans Christian visited Greyfriars spinning room. There, the beakey old crones told tales that made mountains of fear rise from the deep seabed of Hans Christian's imagination.

His pale eyes were his grandmother's eyes, his fantasies of lost wealth inherited from her. She curried and combed him; she soaped and curled his golden hair. When he needed to look smart, she tied a bow of black cloth around his neck.

He acquired his vanity and pride from her, his hunger for acceptance, his courage against all odds. From her he learned to take harsh words and change them into bouquets of compliments. He learned from her that the razor cuts of life could be called a clean shave, if only one told the story properly.

THE BOG KING'S DAUGHTER

◇——··——◇

Of all the things Hans Christian liked about Greyfriars
Hospital, he particularly liked the food he got there.
Once, promised a tasty morsel, he followed an attendant
inside the most frightening building of all, the one where
the lunatics were kept, the broken souls who really did
howl at the moon.

Hans Christian hadn't gone far when he heard a
voice singing on the other side of a door. He knew he
shouldn't stop in this place where madness raced like
blood through the veins of the walls, but he couldn't
help himself. He knelt, peering through a chink. There
he saw a woman clothed only in her hair, her pale skin
like the underbelly of a frog. Without warning, she
leaped from her pile of straw and threw herself at the

door, *shhrrriiiieeeeekkkking*. Fear pressed Hans Christian to the floor. But no matter how flat he made himself, the thin arm of the madwoman snaked down, her fingers writhing, raking the back of Hans Christian's jacket.

Within moments, the attendant rushed up and rescued him. Hans Christian raced home, sucking air through his great nose, his fine hair flying wildly in the wind, his wooden clogs clomping with each footfall.

And when he safely reached the shelter of his family's room, he dared not poke even his big toe out into the world again, until night gave way to morning and he could rejoice at being spared to live another day.

THE SWEETHEARTS

At Carstens School, Sara-who-was-eight attended classes with her brothers. Sara wished to learn arithmetic to be a good milkmaid. Hans Christian loved her. He saw roses blooming in her cheeks; he saw fairies playing in the looping ribbons of her curls. Someday she would live with him in a glass castle.

Hans Christian-who-was-six drew pictures of palaces. He confided to Sara the secret of his birth, that he'd been stolen from his cradle, that his true parents were noble, and they were coming shortly to claim him.

And then he admitted to learning these truths from an angel with swan wings and a voice like the river, an angel with blooming cheeks and curls a bit like Sara's.

When she turned her back on him, he hardly noticed the first nick of her knife, so transfixed was he by the swing of her fickle curls. But when she told her brothers that he was crazy like his grandfather, the blade penetrated like an icicle. It entered his heart, turned it cold.

His grandmother held him as he wept that afternoon. To calm him, she told Hans Christian that a visitor to Odense had heard him singing and had praised his voice, a voice clover sweet, a voice like warm honey the admirer had said. His grandmother knew how to melt the frost in his young heart.

But Hans Christian never trusted the little milkmaid again.

THE COMET

Hans Christian's father laughed, walking with his boy in the woods on that jonquil morning, discussing the comet in scientific terms with Hans Christian and a companionable cricket. The child measured his height against a beech-tree, he sailed a leaf boat on the popply river, he wove a crown from wildflowers, and he used a burdock leaf for a rain hat when fat drops drummed down in a sudden shower. His father shared the shelter of the leaf, his free arm wrapped around the curved back of his boy. They sniffed the damp air together and shook out their leaf with the emerging sun, watching raindrops sparkle around them like so many soap bubbles. Hans Christian's father answered the boy's every question about the comet, promising, promising, the world would not come to an end.

And it didn't.

THE UGLY DUCKLING

From Ane-Marie he got his astonishing length, from his father a nervous hunger. He spoke and a sweet, slurry sound emerged from his lips; he sang and swans treaded water to hear him.

His nose hooked down from his broad forehead; his hooded eyes seemed small in his homely face. But they were lively eyes, recording everything around him.

All his limbs were loose and long. His hands long, his fingers long, his feet and his toes long.

He met sometimes with ridicule, sometimes with indulgent smiles. He carried his genius like a slender bottle of champagne, its silent fizz stopped up, but determined.

And when he met with kindness, he became beautiful.

SOMETHING

◇ ∷ ◇

The first time Hans Christian stepped inside Odense Theater, he gaped at the flushed and giddy audience surrounding him.

But once he'd witnessed the singspiel and the vaudeville of Ludvig Holberg, once he'd heard the rustle of bright costumes and seen shadows vanquished by the shining footlights, once the cheekiness of clever words infected him, his world popped open like a milkweed pod, and something silver and fine came spilling out.

What Father Does
Is Always Right

The parcel arrived in their cramped room. Hans Christian's father fingered the slippery silk and studied his stock of shoe leather, selecting the perfect butter-soft piece for the soles. If he could make the slippers sturdy enough, flattering enough, the Andersens could move out of their crowded room on Monk's Mill Street and into the country, to a squire's estate, where a rent-free cottage and a tiny garden and a green cow pasture would guide them happily through the remainder of their days.

The little band of Andersens breathed their dreams of cuckoos, and flowers, and sunshine into the emerging shoes. When Hans Christian's father snipped the last thread, the boy peered closely at the finished work and smiled. His father spread a kerchief on the bed and arranged the slippers, tying them up tenderly.

But when Hans Christian's father returned from his appointment at the manor, his empty hands, clenched in anger, told everything: How the lady had barely glanced at the slippers before rejecting them. How she had screamed that the shoemaker had ruined her silk. In a boiling fury, Hans Christian's father had destroyed his work, slashing the shoes to ribbons before the lady's eyes.

He arrived home crushed, inconsolable.

Hans Christian, in bed that night, felt the old world crack. And crumble. And tumble away.

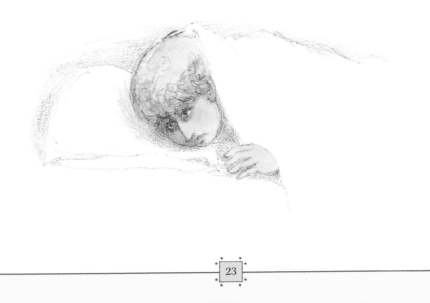

A Drop of Water

After they lost their chance at the house in the country, the Andersens' taste for shoe leather dried up. Hans Christian's father read the newspapers and worshipped Napoleon. And the family had little to eat.

Hans Christian's father had marched as a piper in the Odense regiment for as long as the boy could remember. Now, as his parents quarrelled, he learned that his father would become a real soldier, in the army of Napoleon. Hans Christian gazed at his father in awe.

The family received one thousand thalers for Hans Christian's father to go to war in place of a rich farmer's boy. The day the new recruits departed, his father bent over him. Parched and fevered, Hans Christian dozed in his father's bed, his body spotted with measles. All the ghouls he had met in the spinning-room tales came to warm themselves by the fire of his skin. Hans Christian feared these evil spirits would follow his father to war and reached for him, to warn him.

But the drums called from the street, and Hans Christian's father was suddenly gone, a single drop in the vast sea of Napoleon's army.

THE STEADFAST TIN SOLDIER

◇─ ∴ ─◇

He never fought a single battle. Hans Christian's disillusioned father came home after a two-year absence, his time in Napoleon's service made bitter by retreat and loss of a giant portion of Denmark. He held up his head, kept his back column straight, but when Hans Christian rested his ear on his father's chest, he could hear the rattle of broken pieces.

THE ICE MAIDEN

In the winter, frost flicked its tongue over the window-panes of the Andersens' little room and gazed in at them, hungrily.

"Look," Hans Christian's father said, "there is the ice maiden. Do you see her? She is reaching her hands out to me."

Frightened by the image on the glass, Hans Christian warmed a coin over the stove and pressed it against the pane, melting the ice maiden away, leaving a perfect circle through which to view the frigid streets of Odense.

GRIEF

◇—┄—◇

Hans Christian's father slept often and deeply. When he woke, he shouted orders to comrades. He battled ghosts and the devil. Ane-Marie sent Hans Christian running to the wise woman in Ejby, two miles from their room on Monk's Mill Street, past St. Knut's Church.

Fear made him stretch his legs to full stride, until, doubled over, a stitch in each side, he reached the door of the old crone, Mette Mogensdatter.

"Come here," the crone beckoned. She placed a branch of sacred wood against Hans Christian's chest. "Go home along the river," she instructed. "If your father is to die, you'll meet his ghost along the way."

If before he ran, now Hans Christian flew across the fields, the clang of bells pursuing him like tolling demons. Ever alert, he lurched over the mottled path, startling at every shadow.

Arriving home at last to the yellow cottage, Hans Christian told Ane-Marie all the crone had said. "But," he assured her, struggling for breath, "I did not see a ghost."

It made no difference. Three nights later, his father died.

THE THORNY PATH

Hans Christian slept on the floor beside Ane-Marie. His father's body reposed in the marriage bed. A cricket chirped. It had come to take a walk with the shoemaker.

Ane-Marie sent the cricket away. "He is dead," she told it.

Hans Christian's father had reached the end of the thorny path. Now it was his son's road to travel. The boy grasped a bouquet of green thistles gathered for his father.

He lay the thistles upon his father's chest and stepped back.

The thistles bloomed.

THE OLD GRAVESTONE

◇——··——◇

Ane-Marie remarried when Hans Christian was thirteen — two years after her husband's death. The step-father presided at table now, a young, brown-eyed master cobbler, whose haughty parents snubbed Hans Christian and his mother.

Ane-Marie took in more and more wash, spending long days in the biting cold river. When Hans Christian brought drink to warm her, the autumn mist glimmered over their heads, like graveyard moonlight.

HIDDEN BUT NOT FORGOTTEN

Privy Councilor Falbe and his wife brought their dinner guests to the garden's edge on perfect summer nights, and there, in secret, behind the green hedge, they would have their dessert, a scrumptious serving of Hans Christian's soaring soprano, as he stood in the river alone, completely at home, balanced on the rock Ane-Marie used for a scrub board.

"LOVELY"

Because they heard him on the shores of the Odense River where the green lawns dipped their dainty feet in the frolicking water, because they fell under his spell, the wealthy of Odense — the ones whose forefathers burned cinnamon on their hearths — sent for Hans Christian to entertain them in their drawing rooms.

He stood under the blazing candles of their chandeliers and a bold fire spread through him, rouging his cheeks, glistening his eyes.

They fed him sweetmeats and fruit, sandwiches and red jelly. They flattered and petted him, they laughed with him, and at him.

Hans Christian accepted their attention like a hungry cat accepts a scrap of meat, a dollop of cream.

He would glide home after those evenings, and when the wealthy thought to pay him, he'd slide the lovely coins through the slit in his little clay bank.

Clink. Clink.

THE PIGGY BANK

"What will become of him?" the neighbors asked Ane-Marie when they learned of Hans Christian's plans to journey to Copenhagen and join the theater.

"He is frightened of the sea," Ane-Marie answered. "He will take one look at Nyborg and the Great Belt and come galloping home."

Hans Christian shook off the gnarled hands of Odense. He ordered the stooped shadows to come forward and walk beside him, refusing to let them trail behind, clinging to his shirttails, holding him back.

"I shall be famous," he promised.

His father had foretold it, insisting his son never do anything against his will; the wise crone had foretold it, reading her coffee grounds and cards; the old women spinning in the poorhouse had foretold it, tilting their heads like small birds, sizing him up with their bright eyes.

"First you have a terribly hard time, and then you become famous," Hans Christian said. It was simple.

Breaking open his piggy bank, he counted out thirteen rigsdaler. Thirteen! A grand sum for a boy who survived on dreams.

The Twelve Passengers

◇——⋮——◇

Ane-Marie's chapped hands folded the clothes into a small bundle.

Mother and son walked together to the town gate. The boy could not board the coach at its usual stop, for he was to be a secret passenger who neither begins nor ends where expected.

Hans Christian sniffed the crisp air of autumn. Words tripped eagerly from his lips and the river strutted and crowed. His grandmother, waiting at the gate, silently memorized her darling boy. Ane-Marie reminded him to eat regularly and say his prayers. Only their damp eyes and tight embraces betrayed how hard it was to let him go.

With the bleat of the postilion horn, *trat tra . . . trat tra,* Hans Christian ducked his head and bent his gangling long legs to climb aboard the coach. Finding a place among his fellow travelers, he waved farewell to the two women he loved most in this world.

And just like that, one story ended and another began.

Afterword

On April 2, 1805, in the town of Odense, on the isle of Funen, in the country of Denmark, Ane-Marie Andersdatter, wife of Hans Andersen, gave birth to a squalling baby boy. The pleased parents named their new son Hans Christian.

Most of the town ignored the poverty-ridden Andersens and their homely infant. As he began to grow, Hans Christian's strangeness often met with ridicule and disdain on the streets of Odense. Yet because of the devotion of his paternal grandmother, the boy believed in himself. He trusted that one day he would be admired and celebrated by countrymen and foreigners alike.

At the age of eleven, Andersen lost his father. His mother soon remarried a man who did not appreciate his fanciful stepson. And so, at the age of fourteen, the naive Hans Christian left home. After a grueling journey, he arrived in the Danish capital of Copenhagen knowing no one. He had only a few rigsdaler in his pocket and no way to make more. Arriving at the end of Denmark's last pogrom, Andersen witnessed in the unfamiliar city streets the aftermath of violence directed against Danish Jews, a sight he would not soon forget.

Sheer stubbornness landed young Andersen a place in the Royal Theater's singing school, but his adolescent voice betrayed him and he soon lost the high notes of his soprano range. He moved next to the Royal ballet, where he performed minor roles until Jonas Collin, a Copenhagen philanthropist, arranged a scholarship for the young man to attend Latin school and receive the education he had missed as a child. Andersen was already seventeen years old; his fellow classmates were eleven and twelve.

Hans Christian Andersen towered above his fellow students, stilt legged, bony armed, stoop shouldered, with a protruding nose, tusk-like teeth, and hooded eyes too small for the rest of his face. Always sensitive to slights and offenses of which there were many, both real and imagined, his faults proclaimed themselves to him as loudly as his talents, making him vulnerable to everything and everyone around him, including his own mercurial self. What a wretched time young Andersen had at Latin school. His classmates alternated between teasing and ignoring him. The headmaster tormented him.

In 1827, at the age of twenty-two, Andersen published one of his poems in a Danish newspaper. The debut of "The Dying Child" brought Andersen his first taste of real public attention. The following year, he passed his examinations, completing his education.

Andersen's mother died in the Odense poorhouse in 1833. If she had lived only a few years longer, she would have witnessed her son's meteoric rise to fame. In 1835, Andersen published his first novel, *The Improvisatore,* and the first four of his tales for children. These works met with popular success, though Danish critics showed little kindness toward them. Andersen had boldly experimented with narration and reviewers didn't know what to make of it. He wrote in Danish, but he wrote as the people spoke, much like Mark Twain would later do in America. With the freshness, the humor, and the beauty of this new approach to storytelling, Andersen transformed the literature of Denmark.

By the time he visited England in 1847, at the age of forty-two, he had become a celebrity. Royalty courted him. He befriended luminaries of the nineteenth century such as Jacob and Wilhelm Grimm, Clara and Robert Schumann, Felix Mendelssohn, Alexandre Dumas, Victor Hugo, Robert and Elizabeth Barrett Browning, and Charles Dickens. He corresponded across the ocean with the likes of Henry Wadsworth Longfellow and Horace Scudder, but he never visited America. One of his dearest friends was lost at sea during an ocean passage, steeling Andersen's determination never to make a cross-Atlantic voyage.

In Copenhagen, Andersen lived in a succession of rented rooms. Though his most productive time fell between 1835 and 1848, he continued to write stories for another twenty-four years and kept a diary to the end of his life, dictating when he grew too weak to write. His tales reflected his fears, his joys, his disappointments, his experiences. The themes of poverty and honor, love and courage, adversity and loss forever tied Andersen's world to his fiction.

Over his fifty-year career, Andersen produced thirty-six plays, six travel books, six novels, hundreds of poems, and about one-hundred and seventy tales and stories. In addition, he was a prodigious correspondent, writing as many as fourteen letters in a single day.

Professor Boyesen, a Norwegian American, was one of the many visitors who made a pilgrimage to Hans Christian Andersen's door. During their visit, Andersen recited from memory *The Ugly Duckling* and afterward declared, "It is the story of my own life. I was myself the despised swan in the poultry-yard, the poet in the house of the Philistines."

Cared for in his last days by the Melchiors, a family of wealthy Danish Jews, Andersen died on August 4, 1875, at the age of seventy. Just as he had dreamed in his impoverished childhood, he had become a favorite of royals, beloved by other writers, cherished by his country, and adored by readers worldwide.

BIBLIOGRAPHY

Andersen, Hans Christian. *Twelve Tales*. Translated by Erik Blegvad. New York: Margaret K. McElderry Books, 1994.

Andersen, Hans Christian. *The Stories of Hans Christian Andersen*. Translated from the Danish by Diana Crone Frank and Jeffrey Frank. Boston: Houghton Mifflin, 2003.

Andersen, Hans Christian. *The Complete Fairy Tales and Stories*. Translated from the Danish by Erik Christian Haugaard. New York: Doubleday & Company, Inc., 1974.

Andersen, Hans Christian. *Eighty Fairy Tales*. Translated from the Danish by R.P. Keigwin. New York: Pantheon Books, 1976.

Andersen, Hans Christian. *The Complete Hans Christian Andersen Fairy Tales*. Edited by Lily Owens. New York: Portland House, 1997.

Andersen, Hans Christian. *The Diaries of Hans Christian Andersen*. Selected and translated by Patricia L. Conroy and Sven H. Rossel. Seattle: University of Washington Press, 1990.

Andersen, Hans Christian. *The Fairy Tale of My Life: An Autobiography*. New York: Paddington Press, 1975.

Andersen, Hans Christian. *The True Story of My Life*. Translated by May Howitt. New York: American-Scandinavian Foundation, 1926.

The Andersen-Scudder Letters. Translations by Waldemar Westergaard. Berkeley: University of California, 1949.

Bain, R. Nisbet. *Hans Christian Andersen: A Biography*. New York: Dodd, Mead, 1954.

Book, Fredrik. *Hans Christian Andersen: A Biography*. Translated from the Swedish by George Schoolfield. Norman: University of Oklahoma Press, 1962.

Bredsdorff, Elias. *Hans Christian Andersen: The Story of His Life and Work*. New York: Noonday Press, Farrar, Straus and Giroux, 1975, 1994.

Burnett, Constance Buel. *The Shoemaker's Son: The Life of Hans Christian Andersen*. New York: Junior Literary Guild/Random House, 1941.

Collin, Hedvig. *Young Hans Christian Andersen*. New York: Viking Press, 1955.

David, Julian. *The Three Hanses*. Boston: Little, Brown and Company, 1942.

Dreslov, Aksel. *A River, A Town, A Poet: A Walk Together with Hans Christian Andersen*. Chester Springs, PA: Skandinavisk Bogforlag, Dufour Editions, {circa 1965}.

Larsen, Svend. *The Life History of Hans Christian Andersen*. Odense: Skandinavisk Bogforlag, 1984.

Proudfit, Isabel. *The Ugly Duckling: Hans Christian Andersen*. New York: Robert M. McBride & Company, 1932.

Reumert, Elith. *Hans Christian Andersen: The Man*. Translated from the Danish by Jessie Brochner. New York: E.P. Dutton, 1954.

Spink, Reginald. *Hans Christian Andersen: The Man and His Work*. Copenhagen: Host & Son, 1972.

Stirling, Monica. *The Wild Swan: The Life and Times of Hans Christian Andersen*. New York: Harcourt, Brace & World, 1965.

Toksvig, Signe. *The Life of Hans Christian Andersen*. London: MacMillan and Co., Ltd., 1933.

Wheeler, Opal. *Hans Andersen: Son of Denmark*. New York: E.P. Dutton & Co., Inc., 1951.

Wullschlager, Jackie. *Hans Christian Andersen: The Life of a Storyteller*. Chicago: University of Chicago Press, 2000.

Illustrator's Note

In our childhood home in Copenhagen in the 1920s, my sister and I read from two leather-bound volumes of *H.C. Andersen's Complete Tales and Fairy Tales* that sat on our parents' bookshelves. In Denmark, Andersen is read by everyone, young and old. My sister and I knew the details of H. C. Andersen's life, and we knew much of his poetry and fairy tales, as well. Certain poems of his were set to music and sung, almost like national anthems, in our school. I am still able to recite bits and pieces of them.

Several times, as an illustrator and a Dane, I have had the great good fortune to illustrate and translate some of Andersen's fairy tales into English. At first, I felt out of my depth, believing they had already been illustrated to perfection long ago, and that I would be foolish to try to do better. Andersen's own choice of illustrator, Vilhelm Pedersen, had produced such lovely pencil drawings for the first fairy tales in 1848 that I was sure I could not do justice to the text. I tried anyway, of course.

Karen Hesse's poetic telling of Andersen's early days has enriched my connection to Andersen enormously, by giving me insight into what I am sure were the very thoughts of his childhood. I only hope my drawings, in the absence of any photos or portraits detailing this period, will give some idea of how his early life, his family, and he, himself, may well have appeared.